Charles Stow

An Iron Creed

Charles Stow

An Iron Creed

ISBN/EAN: 9783337182700

Printed in Europe, USA, Canada, Australia, Japan

Cover: Foto ©Lupo / pixelio.de

More available books at **www.hansebooks.com**

IN FIVE ACTS,

BY

CHARLES STOW.

CHARACTERS:

DAVID DELMONT,.......................... A BANKER
JEM BRAZENCRAFT, *alias* JOHN FAIRLOOK, A PARADOX
BRACE NIGHTHAWK,........................ A FRIEND
FITZ-MASHER DE PUTTIPAYTE................ A LORD
ANGLICE APEBULL,..........................A COPY
DR. STERNLAW,............................. A RABBI
SAM. BOODLEBANG,.........................A CRŒSUS
LOCUST PROMPT,.................... A POLICEMAN
RUTH,......................... DELMONT'S DAUGHTER
MRS. BOODLEBANG.................A TUFT-HUNTER
MRS. ARTHUR,................................A WIDOW
MISS FAWN,...................... AN ORNAMENT
MISS ANGLE,.............................. A TYPE
ALICE,.................................. A CHILD
NANNY,................................. A TREASURE

Time, . THE PRESENT.

Place. . THE GREAT CITY.

AN IRON CREED.

ACT I.

SCENE—A RECEPTION ROOM IN DAVID DELMONT'S HOUSE.

(*Enter* NANNY, *flourishing a duster, and carrying the morning mail.*)

NAN. "The wasterful manner in which you peels pertaters would breed a famine in Ireland." Them's the compliments of the season Master Nickel squeeze dropped inter the kitchen ter perlitely present me, at a quarter to six this blessed mornin'— a hour when all Christian feller citizens, except slavin' Cinderellers is tranquiliforously snorin' the happy hours away. He gits up for fear of losin' a second's daylight. Things in this ere house is drawn closer'n a bride's corsets. Master's so teetotally tight. I don't believe he'd sweat without deductin' it from the water tax, and you couldn't get inter his pockets with a crowbar. More'n half the time there aint nothin' fit for a orthodox heathen to eat, nuther. I've clean forgot whether ham's red, white or blue, and how roast pork smells—and sassengers; fried sassengers! whenever I thinks of them, my mouth waters like I'd been salervated. If it wan't for Miss Ruth, I'd break out and jine the Salvashun Army. But she's a daisy of the female gander, she is. When Dad quit, she took me in and cared for me, and I'll stick by her, even if I have to eat unleveled bread all Christmas week. (*Throws the mail on the writing desk and upsets the ink bottle.*) Now I *am* in for it! (*Hastily mops up the ink with the blotters.*) Heaving's, he's comin' now! (*Stuffs the blotters in the bosom of her dress and begins dusting vigorously.*)

(*Enter* DAVID DELMONT.)

DEL. I think I must try and spare a thousand for that purpose; it is a most commendable one. (*Goes to writing desk.*) What's this? The ink spilled and three sheets of good paper and as many envelopes ruined! Girl, this is your doings. Will you never learn that carelessness leads to extravagance, extravagance to want, want to temptation, and temptation to crime?

NAN. (*Aside.*) And my wages to the poor house.

DEL. Where are all the blotters?

NAN. Please, sir, I used them to blot up the ink with. That's what they're fur, aint it?

DEL. Universal waste and destruction seem to be what you are for.

NAN. I'm sure, sir, I tries to attend to my duties with neatness and dispatch, as the little liver pill labels says.

DEL. You do? And pray, after this fresh illustration, may I make so bold as to ask what you consider your duties?

NAN. Well, I am cook, washer, janitor, chambermaid, stoker, waiter, bootblack, errand boy, snow plow, door tender, chores, mop, lady's maid, and I expect to be nuss some day.

DEL. Don't let your impertinence presume too much on my daughter's favor. That will do.

NAN. (*Aside.*) I should rather say it would.

DEL. Learn to do one thing well and carefully at a time.

NAN. How can I, sir, when I'se expected to do everything all the time?

DEL. I'll give you a few practical lessons, by charging you with some of the results of your carelessness.

NAN. (*Aside.*) If you finds anything valerable about my pusson, I'll go halvers with you.

DEL. Some one is ringing ; go see who it is. (*Exit NANNY*).

(*Opens ledger and looks at it.*) This won't answer. Over a hundred thousand dollars outstanding that's overdue. Times look ominous, and values are shrinking. I must push collections.

(*Enter RABBI STERNLAW.*)

RAB. Good morrow, David.

DEL. Welcome, Doctor. What news from the world's broad vineyard, to-day ?

RAB. There are very many worthy laborers still sorely in need, and I must add, so many of the true faith, that those who follow after strange gods should look to them first for succor.

DEL. Not so, Doctor ; for all the virtuous poor are God's children. There is no creed or nationality in want and suffering. Even the Gentile in distress should be the rich man's brother.

RAB. At least it cannot be denied that you secretly practice what you preach.

DEL. I do so, Doctor, because it is the will of Him for whom I hold the means in trust ; and secretly from all but you, because it saves me from being overrun by swindling beggars, social tramps and cheap philanthropists—the last of whom I dread the most.

RAB. Would that I could equally interest you, my noble friend, in the grand and holy scheme of redeeming the Promised Land, and building up therein a New Jerusalem. You are qualified for it, and if you will but consent to assume the leadership, you shall rank in all after chronicles with Israel's most glorious redeemers—the mighty Moses of a second Exodus.

DEL. Dreams ; idle dreams, my friend. A delusive vision, born of a too literal application of prophetic teachings. Gaze not, with vain longings, from Nebo's heights upon a kingdom you can never reach. This home of freedom is our promised land, and here the New Jerusalem, in which to erect a living temple ; far more glorious and enduring than even that of Solomon—one founded on the eternal rock of patriotism and good actions. Hither let it be our aim to gather all our suffering, persecuted brethren, from out the house of the Old World's despotic bondage, into a land flowing with the spiritual milk and honey of toleration, enlightened progress and universal protection. This is a practical age, and we must keep abreast of it. Here is a case in point—a heart-rending appeal from the robbed and persecuted Jews in Russia. Sit down and look it over, and let us consider the best means of succoring them. (*Hands him a paper.*)

(*Enter NANNY with a coal scuttle.*)

NAN. A lady and a kid to see you, sir.

DEL. A kid?

NAN. Yes : her'n, you know. Here they be. (*Exit NANNY*.)

(*Enter MRS. ARTHUR and Alice.*)

DEL. You are welcome, Madam. (*Hands her a chair.*)

MRS. A. I fear, sir. I shall prove an unwelcome, as I am a most unfortunate visitor.

DEL. Is it not the fashion of the world to welcome the misfortunes of others ? But what can I do for you ?

MRS. A. I am your debtor, sir.

DEL. There must be some mistake ; I do not remember ever having seen you before.

MRS. A. I am Mrs. George Arthur.

DEL. Ah, indeed ! Let me see (*looks at ledger*). Yes ; you are right. Here it is ; George Arthur, note of b nd for $800.00.

MRS. A. He died last week, sir.

DEL. Dead ! That's bad for both of us.

MRS. A. He meant honestly by you, sir, and had saved up a part of the money to pay you, but it all went during his long sickness. He told me on his dying bed, that when he was hurt in the mill and unable to work for so long, but for you we would have lost our little home, and he charged me to pay a debt so sacred. If you will but kindly give me time, I'll try and sell the place and do so.

DEL. Sell the place ? Nonsense ! Sheer nonsense ! But you women folk know nothing about business. The fact is, there was an unsettled account between us. Your husband did me a service for which I owe you something. Excuse me a moment, and I will look it up. (*Examines ledger and writes.*)

ALICE. (*To the Rabbi.*) Mr. Moses, where is your fish-pole, and the tomb stones with printing and these things (*forming an X by a gesture*), that's in the big picture book at home ?

RAB. My child, I am not Moses, nor nearly so great and good a man.

ALICE. Then you must be Mr. Santa Claus.

RAB. Wrong again, my bright little Yankee guesser.

ALICE. No? Well, then, you're a real nice, good old grandfather, aren't you? If I had one I should want him to look just like you.

RAB. I am but a lonely old man, my dear, with neither children, nor grandchildren.

ALICE. My, that's too bad, you dear old thing you! I'm awfully sorry, but I'll tell you what to do. Come over to our house and we'll play grandpa, and have such a lovely time.

RAB. I should much like to, my kind little friend.

MRS. A. Alice, you must not trouble the gentleman.

RAB. Not at all; I assure you, Madam. She delights me.

DEL. (To Mrs. Arthur). I find, Madam, that the accounts so nearly balance, the difference is not worth speaking of. There is your husband's note. (Hands her a folded paper.)

MRS. A. (Opens the note). But, sir, you have made a mistake. Here is a hundred dollar bill, besides.

DEL. Is there? Well, I deserve to lose it for my carelessness. So, keep it, and say no more about it.

MRS. A. (Falling on her knees). Oh, sir, may the God of the widow and orphan bless and reward you.

ALICE. (Kneeling beside her mother). Mamma, may I pray for the good gentleman, too?

DEL. Rise, Madam. I cannot abide that you should kneel to such as I. You owe me no thanks. All I ask—and that most earnestly—is that you never mention this trifling matter; for if you do, I shall have every needy person in town plucking at my mantle.

(Enter RUTH.)

MRS. A. I most solemnly promise never to mention it, except in my prayers, and to my own grateful heart.

RUTH. Why, father, you are holding quite a levee to-day.

DEL. Receiving tribute; that is all, my child. Mrs. Arthur, this is my scapegrace daughter. The wife of an old friend, Ruth, but lately lost to us.

RUTH. I hope, that we shall be friends, too, and I sincerely sympathize with you in your great affliction.

MRS. A. Your sweet face proves it, and, surely, such a father should have an angel daughter to comfort him.

DEL. Madam, remember!

MRS. A. If I remain, I shall forget myself. Come, Alice.

(Enter NANNY, carrying a mop.)

NAN. Mr. Nighthawk's complaints, sir, and are you in?

DEL. Yes. (Aside.) Though I fear I shall be out if I have much more to do with him. (Exit NANNY.)

MRS. A. (Going). Good morning.

DEL. and RUTH. Good morning.

ALICE. By-by, everybody, and dear Mr. Grandpa, don't you forget my invitation.

(Enter NIGHTHAWK, in haste. Runs against Alice.)

NIGHT. Get out of the way, you little monkey.

ALICE. Sir, I'm a little lady, and that's a good deal more than you will ever be: you big Mr. Crowley, you. (Exit MRS. ARTHUR and ALICE.)

NIGHT. I beg pardon, Miss Delmont.

RUTH. I think the apology is due rather to the younger lady, Mr. Nighthawk.

NIGHT. Then let me extend it to both. (Aside.) Curse her; how she cuts me whenever she gets the chance. I'll make her pay for it some day.

RUTH. Father, haven't you forgotten something this morning?

DEL. Not that I know of, my child.

RUTH. (Standing before him and puckering up her mouth). What, nothing?

DEL. Thanks for the tempting reminder, and I will become your debtor, by thus discharging my forgotten debt. (Kisses her.)

RUTH. You shall be handsomely rewarded for such a gallant speech as that. There. (Handing him a bouquet.)

DEL. They are very beautiful, my child; as pure and fragrant as the giver's love. But you will spoil me by such extravagant remembrances. These costly luxuries are not for me.

NIGHT. (Aside). What an infernal old skin-flint.

RAB. (Aside). What a strange, yet noble paradox.

RUTH. Why, father, you deserve the best and brightest things of all the earth.

4

DEL. I have them here (*embracing her*), my child. Otherwise my ways are frugal and my wants are few. But I have much to do; so I'll excuse you now.

RUTH. Rather a curt dismissal; but I will pardon you if you will let me take the Doctor with me.

DEL. I think I can safely trust him with you.

RUTH. (*Going*). Come, then, Doctor, and share my banishment (*aside to him*), and you shall tell me more of the glorious wonders of the New Jerusalem.

RAB. Would that I had a million such sympathizers.

(*Exit* RUTH *and* RABBI).

DEL. (*Putting the flowers in a vase*). How emblematic of the bloom and beauty of her young life ; and, yet, how soon they will fade and droop, as did her gentle mother.

NIGHT. Now that the coast is clear, I would pay sacrifice to the Golden Calf of Gotham.

DEL. Inflict your idolatrous wit, sir, on your brother heathens. I do not relish it.

NIGHT. (*Aside*). The insolent Dead Sea shark. But I am run to earth, and must bolt his wormwood if I would finger his shekels. (*Aloud*). Don't be so infernally crusty, Delmont, I've business with you.

DEL. (*Aside*). The Prodigal's clean shorn again. (*Aloud*). I presume you have called to pay me something. It is time.

NIGHT. Is this a place where people come to pay ? I thought it was a shop for borrowers only.

DEL. Then, sir, you are clearly in the wrong shop, for I have naught to lend.

NIGHT. Confound it, be a decent and accommodating Crœsus for once, cant you ? I must have money.

DEL. Then you must get it elsewhere.

NIGHT. My honor is at stake.

DEL. So is my capital, and it is not business to stake that against your honor.

NIGHT. You already have ample security of mine in your hands.

DEL. Not a vulgar fraction of a margin, sir. I have already advanced more than is prudent.

NIGHT. Do you then refuse to help me, after all I have paid you ?

DEL. Excuse me, sir, you have paid me nothing.

NIGHT. But I mean to.

DEL. I can't discount an empty promise on the exchange, sir.

NIGHT. But you can charge double Shylock usury on promises secured.

DEL. Can I ? Pay me the bare principal on what I have already loaned you, and I will forego the interest.

NIGHT. That's only a cheap bluff. But what other treatment can a gentleman expect from the son of a rag picking Jew ?

DEL. Your father was a gentleman. He deserved the threadbare title, and I have been liberal with you on his account. Mine was both poor and humble; but which one, think you, has most occasion to be proudest of his son ?

NIGHT. Good fortune has made the Jew most arrogant. You forget yourself. You was born on a dunghill.

DEL. And you wallow in one ; a reckless spendthrift, besmeared with the filth of every excess.

(*Enter* NANNY, *with a rolling pin*).

NIGHT. You lie, you vampire, and I'll prove it on your swinish carcass, before I leave you! (*Rushes at Delmont with uplifted cane. NANNY interferes and knocks him down with the Rolling pin*).

NAN. (*Standing over Nighthawk and pointing the rolling pin at him*). Stir but a toe-nail, and I'll blow your brains out.

[CURTAIN.]

ACT II.

A DRAWING ROOM IN BOODLEBANG'S HOUSE (DANCING MUSIC HEARD IN THE DISTANCE).

(*Enter* JEM BRAZENCRAFT, *alias* JOHN FAIRLOOK.)

FAIR. (*Inspecting himself in a mirror.*) Not an uncommon sight, the Devil in a dress suit; but so rarely such a thorough-paced devil of a devil thus disguised, that I am really quite interested in you, Jem Brazencraft, *alias* Mr. John Fairlook. You was born a gambler, forger and thief: your father, a felon; your mother, the frailest and silliest of dupes. and, yet, you are a very honest sort of fellow; that is, with yourself to yourself; and something of an artist withal; for, while fate fashioned your inside, you have made the outside fairly shine and dazzle with the veneer of polished respectability—at once society's worst enemy and greatest ornament. Posing with consummate and elegant assurance on a volcano's quaking summit. All the excitement of the stage with the spice of danger added. You are a most fascinating and villianous success, Jem Brazencraft. Permit me to offer you the assurance of my most distinguished consideration. (*Taking pack of cards from his pocket.*) Let me get rid of these familiars; they have served their purpose well. (*Throws cards into the fire.*)

(*Enter* NIGHTHAWK.)

Ah! brother blackleg, all hail! Your dirty fingers itch to fondle their share of this night's plunder. Well, there it is. (*Hands him money.*)

NIGHT. You are devilish complimentary.

FAIR. And candid, as well; as my Lord Duffer, whom you have just helped me to so artistically skin, would roundly swear to, did he but know you.

NIGHT. The truth should not be told at all times.

FAIR. Granted; but to tell it semi-occasionally, my squeamish pal, capper and associate scoundrel, mightily refreshes a man, when he has to live a lie all the time.

NIGHT. It never refreshes me.

FAIR. You never tried it.

NIGHT. I have something more profitable to talk about, if you will clap a stopper on that blistering tongue of yours long enough to hear it.

FAIR. Then Truth is muzzled. Lie on.

NIGHT. Jack, what would you give me were I to put a million dollars in your hands?

FAIR. This piece of excellent advice, you bankrupt satan: Don't at'empt to play jackass and villian at the same time. The characters wont couple. The one would kick the other's brains out—that is, if it has any.

NIGHT. Blackguard and chaff me all you will, but I can do it, all the same, if you will let me steer you.

FAIR. And by what means?

NIGHT. Marriage.

FAIR. Marriage! Ha, ha! I marry? My maudlin match-maker, hereafter woo not Widow Cliquot so hotly. Your weak head can't withstand her seductive blandishments. Why, man, the average woman disgusts me, and as for the rare exceptions; well, they may serve as playthings. You've got an awful still on.

NIGHT. If you were in your sober senses, you'd see that a million dollars, whose only encumbrance is a rare beauty and a wedding ring, is not the sort of a pearl to cast before swine.

FAIR. And yet, you see, I am not hog enough to swallow it. Why don't you put the ring in your own snout?

NIGHT. Because I can't. Her father is onto me, and she dislikes me.

FAIR. Why, then, would you be the Buckingham to buckle this great fortune on my back? You are utterly incapable of doing even me a disinterested favor. Plainly, what's your lay?

NIGHT. Revenge and profit.

FAIR. So doubly natural a motive that you compel my confidence.

NIGHT. I have good reason to hate both her father and herself.

FAIR. You must have, to propose such a son-in-law and husband for them.

NIGHT. Besides, I could at once genteely rob and torture him. I know her disposition well. She is romantic, high-spirited, impulsive, ingenuous and affectionate. You are just the sort of man to catch her fancy, and, with my assistance, I am dead sure you can capture her and bag the million. But if we succeed I am to have ten per cent

FAIR. Of which?

NIGHT. Why, the swag, of course.

FAIR. Oh! that's very reasonable for you. But who is this gilded paragon?

NIGHT. The only child of Delmont, the millionaire Jew banker.

FAIR. I know him slightly.

NIGHT. And shall know her well to-night, if you but will, for she is here.

FAIR. But hold! I have some orthodox compunctions in this matter, and my conscience pricks me. Surely you would not have a Christian; one who pays highest auction prices for a pew, turn apostate and wed with Israel?

NIGHT. I'd have you turn an honest penny one hundred million times, and, as you are situated, you'd better do it.

FAIR. Well, I'll risk turning a speculative eye upon her, and *when* I marry, you shall be well paid for acting as best man, my thrifty stool-pigeon to Mercury and Venus.

(*Enter* Mrs. BOODLEBANG, Miss FAWN, Miss ANGLE, Lord DEPUTTIPAYTE, BOODLEBANG and APEBULL.)

APE. (*To Lord DeP.*) And so you focused the blazing sunbeams in the enraged tiger's glaring orb with your intrepid eye-glass and cooked his beastly brains?

DEP. Y-a-a-s, by Jove, and ate them afterwards. Ra-a-ther gamey, but wildly animating luncheon, you know. Egad, it made me feel so dooced tigerish, that my nails grew four inches in as many hours.

APE. What extraordinary aristowatic nerve, and stomach. (*Aside.*) I shall pwoceed to experiment on a tom-cat forthwith.

BOODLEBANG. You're sure it wan't a wild buffalo calf, my lud?

MRS. B. What a vulgar idea. Don't you suppose a real lord knows a calf when he sees one?

BOOD. The lord knows. Possibly, if he has read "As in a Looking Glass."

MRS. B. (*Aside.*) Boodlebang, you're an untutored savage.

BOOD. (*Aside.*) And my darling toady, you're a bigger fool than ever he is.

(*Enter* RUTH—*Bows distantly to Nighthawk.*)

FAIR. (*To Nighthawk.*) Who is that pensive-eyed goddess? She looks and moves as I should imagine Queen Esther might have done.

NIGHT. So, so! The biter bitten at the first facing. That, my boy, is the chief encumbrance to Delmont's millions.

FAIR. Introduce me.

NIGHT. That won't do. It would be sending you to hopeless protest. Get Mrs. Boodlebang to play the fat propitious angel and throw open the doors of paradise to you.

Miss A. (*To Lord DeP.*) You heroic creature, you! After that tiger episode I am positively afraid of you.

DEP. I nevah eat ladies, you know.

APE. (*Aside.*) He is not fond of sweetmeats—I must taboo toffy hereafter.

DEP. But, by Jove, I'm awfully dangerous to the softer sex, you know.

RUTH. And the softer, the more dangerous, I imagine.

DEP. Y-a-a-s. For example: when I was special envoy at Algiers, I got into the seraglio by means of a golden key. They were a *harem-scarum* lot there.

APE. Capital, by Jove!

BOODLE. Ring the bell.

MRS. B. (*Aside.*) I'd like to wring your nose!

DEP. And all the 1117 sultanas fell dead in love with me.

MISS FAWN. As they naturally would.

DEP. Y-a-a-s; but unfortunately for the dear, susceptible houris, I could not reciprocate. The delicate status of our diplomatic relations forbade it, you know; and it broke all their tender hearts.

Miss F. Did they die?

DEP. Y-a-a-s, every one of them.

APE. What, all?

DEP. All! 'Pon honah, all!

Miss F. Poor dears.

MISS ANGLE. How romantic.

FAIR. I pity the poor sultan most.

BOODLE. Not because he got rid of so many wives? The lucky dog.

FAIR. Oh, no! But furnishing crape for such a wholesale funeral must have broke him, too.

BOODLE. Cork up your sympathy, Fairlook. There's just *one* family expense that often brings joy on earth, if not in heaven.

DEP. (*Aside.*) That charming female native with the dreamy eyes seems to stand in awe of me. I must reward her modest diffidence, and at the same time hook her. (*Aloud, to Ruth.*) My deah Miss—Aw—Miss—Miss—Weally, I beg pardon, but I seem to have forgotten your name, you know.

RUTH. Delmont; if it can be worth your lordship's while to remember so insignificant a thing

DEP. Thanks. You may not think it, but, weally, Miss—Miss—Aw!—Miss Denmark, I'm actually delighted to know you, you know.

RUTH. I did not know that it was in any way essential for a lord to know much of anything, you know.

FAIR. (*Aside.*) She's bright as well as beautiful. I'm thawing fast.

BOODLE. It isn't, you know—They can hire it, and that's easier, don't-yer-know.

FAIR. That's a valuable hint for you, Apebull; you'd better get some.

APE. But, my deah fellah, we can't procure the genuine article in this blarsted country, you know.

FAIR. Oh, yes, plenty of it.

APE. And where, pray.

FAIR. At the asylum for hopeless imbeciles, my dear fellow, don't you know.

DEP. My deah Miss—Miss—Aw!—Demlot; before I came to America I had an ideah—

RUTH. Did you bring it with you?

DEP. (*Aside.*) How refreshingly unsophisticated she is, to be sure. (*Aloud.*) Why, certainly. I had an idea, you know, that the native ladies in New York painted their faces, wore red horse cloths, and stuck feathers in their hair.

RUTH. Some of them do paint. I have heard.

MISS ANGLE. What a horrid slander.

RUTH. And as to our wearing the feathers, it would not seem more odd, would it, than is the fact that most of the English geese we see here have none?

DEP. Weally, now, don't they? By Jove, that's very odd, you know. Do they pluck them before they are sent over.

RUTH. Not always.

FAIR. But some of them are plucked mighty clean after they get here; eh, Nighthawk?

DEP. I am also highly gratified to note a twemendous effort in your best society to pattern after our noble selves. Take Apebull, for instance. Though sometimes a little off in accent, attitude and manners, and crude in dress, as a whole, he would not disgrace either my tailor or my ancestral halls.

APE. O, my Lord, you flatter me. (*Aside.*) This is inexpwessibly gwatifying and encouraging. I'll order another pair of twousers to-morrow.

RUTH. You outdo his lordship then, Mr. Apebull, for imitation is the sincerest flattery, you know.

DEP. Y-a-a-s. He, and the other fellahs like him, are true refomahs and deserve encouragement.

RUTH. I am happy to be able to assure your lordship that all sensible people appreciate them at their full value.

DEP. That's wight. But, aw! though you are such a chawming magnet, my deah Miss—Miss—Aw!—Delsot, I shall have to tear myself away and mingle with the common herd that impatiently longs for me. But may I beg permission to call on you?

RUTH. Oh! my lord, you overwhelm me, and are by far too gracious. We could scarcely hope, and never dare to look, for so much condescension from nobility.

DEP. (*Aside.*) Egad! she's winged. (*Aloud.*) Don't mention it. A great pleasah, I assure you. So, till then (*throwing her a kiss*), adieu.

(*Exit* DEP. *followed by* Miss FAWN.)

APE. Aw! Miss Delmont, allow me to congratulate you.

RUTH. And why, sir, pray?

APE. For having made such a palpable impression on his lordship.

RUTH. Did I, indeed? I was not aware of it. (*Looking at her hands.*) I do not discover any dough on my fingers. How very, very soft he is, to be sure. I know of but one thing softer.

APE. Your heart, Miss Delmont?

RUTH. No! The heads of his American imitators, Mr. Apebull.

APE. I shall certainly report your unkind remarks to his lordship, Miss Delmont.

RUTH. Thank you. I could not have suggested a more fitting messenger for the purpose.

(*Exit* APEBULL.)

FAIR. (*To Mrs. Boodlebang.*) Won't you favor me with an introduction to Miss Delmont?

MRS. B. What? It's the first time, in all the years I've known you, you ever asked me for such a thing. I've positively had to drag you into a nodding acquaintance with any petticoat, and now you actually throw yourself at one. What's come over you?

FAIR. You see, my dear Madam, I'm improving under your gentle and winning influence.

MRS. B. Oh, get out; you frozen stick of taffy! You're in for it, at last, and I'm more than willing to shove you in deeper. So, come along.

(*Enter* APEBULL.)

APE. His Lordship wants you, Boodlebang.

BOODLE. I hope he don't want to borrow anything.

MRS. B. You ought to feel yourself honored if he does.

BOODLE. I'm cussedly afraid it would be dishonored if he did.

(*Exit* APEBULL *and* BOODLEBANG.)

MRS. B. Miss Delmont I want to introduce you to the North Pole; otherwise known as Mr. John Fairlook, and if he treats you as cooly as he does my other lady friends you'd best send for your seal-skin, or your teeth will be chattering inside of five minutes. Now, I must go and look after his Lordship. So, adoo.

(*Exit* MRS. BOODLEBANG.)

FAIR. An icy slander, I assure you, Miss Delmont. I am not in the least rigid. I simply discriminate.

RUTH. Am I to regard that as a special compliment, Mr. Fairlook? If so, I fear I shall receive you so cooly, in turn, that you will have to send for your overcoat. I detest compliments, and give you warning that I shall not like you if you pay them.

FAIR. Truly, a most fair warning; but, may I ask you, will you like me if I do not pay them?

RUTH. I can't promise quite so much as that; but I will try very hard not to dislike you.

FAIR. Even on that small encouragement, I am prepared to solemnly assure you that I never paid one in the whole course of my life, unless it was to make faces at my nurse.

RUTH. How could that be a compliment?

FAIR. She was so magnificently homely, you see.

RUTH. I may catch you making faces at me, sir.

FAIR. You cannot beguile me into a fatal compliment even with such a tempting opening. I want to make neither faces nor compliments, but friends. I have the honor of a slight acquaintance with your father, and I pay no idle compliment in assuring you that I respect and esteem him most highly.

RUTH. O, you may compliment him all you please, for I like that; and, if you really like him, I fear I shall be indiscreet enough to like you.

FAIR. A most acceptable proof that "like begets like."

RUTH. Now, had you substituted charming for acceptable, you would have been like to stultify yourself.

FAIR. Another proof that the truth should not be spoken at all times. But, Miss Delmont, you won't mistake it for a compliment if I express my keen enjoyment of the manner in which you plucked that English goose?

RUTH. Did you, indeed?

FAIR. How could I do otherwise, for am I not an American of Americans, Miss Delmont?

RUTH. And I am proud of you for being one, Mr. Fairlook.

FAIR. Truly, so then am I; though I don't remember to have ever been particularly proud of myself before.

RUTH. Beware, Mr. Fairlook!

FAIR. What for? Of being an American? I thought only your enemies should beware of that.

RUTH. I am the friend of every true American.

FAIR. Then, most truly, we are friends; for you have said it.

(*Enter* BOODLEBANG.)

BOODLE. Miss Ruth, you know you promised me the next dance, and I'm not going to be cheated out of the loveliest lass in the whole lot.

RUTH. With pleasure, if Mr. Fairlook will kindly excuse me.

9

FAIR. Certainly; though I can't sincerely add, with pleasure. (*Aside.*) The old marplot. I'd like to cut a pigeon-wing on his tombstone.

RUTH. (*Aside.*) I really think I should like to have him for a friend. (*Music is heard.*) Oh, what a delicious hop waltz! Come, Mr. Boodlebang.

BOODLE. The deuce it is! I thought it was a Virginia Reel. I'm no flea, you see. I can't hop; so we'll have to postpone hostilities.

RUTH. I'm so sorry. It's a *real* disappointment, you know.

BOODLE. (*Imitating Apebull.*) Capital, by Jove!

NIGHT. (*To Fairlook.*) Well, what's the verdict? Do you go in for the million?

FAIR. I never once thought of it.

NIGHT. That settles it! You'll marry her; but you must go about it honorably.

FAIR. Honorably! That word must have a strange flavor in your mouth.

NIGHT. I use it practically, not sentimentally.

FAIR. How so?

NIGHT. You must formally ask her father for her hand.

FAIR. But will he not refuse me? Am I not a Christian?

NIGHT. Turn Jew, then.

FAIR. But, if he still refuses?

NIGHT. Then marry her in spite of him. You will have fully convinced her of your honor and sincerity and thus win her confidence. That gained, the rest will follow. Without it you will fail. I know her.

FAIR. You are so wise that I shall call you Owl, instead of Nighthawk, hereafter. Well, if I ever find the time, I may think of it.

NIGHT. (*Aside.*) Yes, and you'll do it, too; and carry the bag for me, in spite of all your insolence.

(*Enter* APEBULL.)

APE. (*Wildly.*) I had her all to myself in the conservatory, and was getting on swimmingly; when, just as I was about to pop, that blawsted, bwazen Ishmaelite came in and cut me clean out, as quick as he would snip off a sample of shoddy with his vulgah shears. Curse him and all his thieving tribe!

MISS ANGLE. Why, what can be the matter, my dear Mr. Apebull? Who are you talking about?

(*Enter* Mrs. BOODLEBANG, Miss FAWN and Lord DEP.)

APEBULL. A dastardly, devilish, dirty, depwaved, defwading Pharisee!

DEP. What's the wumpus?

APE. They're all alike and ought to be dwiven out of the country, like hogs, at the bayonet's point; their stealings confiscated, and bonfires made of their houses, to celebrate the joyful occasion.

MISS A. That would be too good treatment for some of them, I know.

MISS F. So it would—the impudent graduates from slums and slop shops.

BOODLE. By thunder, this is my house, and I want to know wh t all this means!

APE. Means! It means that I'd like to hang every—

FAIR. (*Seizing Apebull.*) Stop, you idiotic blackguard! Not another word or, I swear, I'll strangle you!

RUTH. Hold, Mr. Fairlook! This is my affair. (*Facing Apbull, Miss A. and Miss F.*) And who are you, that you should dare to thus infamously and falsely defame and revile a great nation? Kings, conquerors, heroes. prophets and poets; ages before your savage ancestors made their lairs in northern swamps and thickets; shivered, half naked, in the raw skins of other beasts; fed on offal, and robbed and murdered in the name of mist-born demons; slaughter, their pastime, and civilization, their abhorrence. I am a Jewess! I glory in it! And I will defend my people!

[CURTAIN.]

ACT III.

SCENE, *same as in Act I.*

(*Enter* NANNY, *with a carver in her hand.*)

NAN. Miss. Ruth's got 'em, and she's a goner. Ever since I seed the noble villian in that ere sweet meller dramer jump, like a heroic bull-frog, from the whirligig bridge into a big cistern and rescue the forlorn maiden from her untimely end, I've had all the symptherms, and (*striking her heart*), I've got 'em down pat. I might as well begin postin' up on the nussin' biz; it's comin', sure. (*Sings the following.*)

[SONG.]

O, luve! luve! luve! you're a very queer thing,
  For gittin' us soft-hearted gals on the string;
The old and the young: though the old 'uns is wust,
  Because the most anxious to take you on trust.

All ages and colors: all sizes and kind;
  You knock 'em all out, even though you be blind;
And even the red-headed gal and white hoss,
  Must agree with the blackest that you are the boss.

Like the skeeter, you've wings, and don't wear any clothes;
  Like him, into everyone your arrer goes.
Like his, too, your jabs, how they itches and smarts;
  He but pizens the skin, while you pizens our hearts.

(*Enter* RUTH.)

O, luve! luve! luve! from what little I've seen,
  I'd as soon smoke a pipe in a fort's magazine,
As trust you; for after the ring there's a show-up,
  Then off comes your blinders, and lor' what a blow-up.

RUTH. You're in high spirits, Nanny. I almost envy you.

NAN. (*Aside.*) Another sympterm! (*Aloud*) Envy the likes of me, Miss. Ruth? Though I admits I is to be envied for having such a splendiferous missus as you is.

RUTH. You are a good girl, Nanny, and I should be very helpless without you.

NAN. I'm sure I tries to be, Miss Ruth, and my heart is right under the sole of your little slipper this very minnit. (*Aside.*) When she talks to me like that, it makes me feel just like the noble villian was ticklin' me all over. (*Aloud.*) But what's the matter with you, Miss Ruth? You seems resless like, and you're off your feed. I don't hear you sing no more, and the way you sighs sometimes is most enough to blow the gas out. You aint gone and caught the dyspepser, has you?

RUTH. Nothing quite so bad as that, I hope, but I do feel unaccountably depressed and melancholy; so much so at times, I am strangely impressed with the idea that something dreadful is about to happen.

NAN. (*Aside.*) That settles it. (*Aloud.*) Cheer up! It may only be a earthquake. I would just like to see anything happen to you, Miss Ruth, I would, when I was in the same ward. Your nerves is on a strike: that's what's the matter. You need bracin' up. Try gin.

RUTH. What a remedy to recommend to a lady.

NAN. That's what Dad always took, and the way it used to raise his speerits was a holy terror to the whole block. What's that?

RUTH. Goodness! What startled you so?

NAN. Bless my sinful soul; the sass is bilin' over!

(*Exit* NANNY, *running.*)

RUTH. A condition which she is in half the time; but, after all, she is a rough diamond, without a flaw, and true as steel. Heigh, ho! I wonder what has become of Mr. Fairlook. It's two whole days since he called. How promptly he championed my cause, and how nobly indignant he looked. True, any gentleman would have done the same, but very few could have done it so well.

(*Enter* DELMONT.)

DEL. Ruth, I am just going to step down and look at that saddle horse you fancied so much. If he is safe and sound, and you will promise to be a very good girl, I may buy him for you.

11

RUTH. Dear father, how good you are to me, and yet, I should enjoy your loving generosity far better, did you but think oftener of your own comfort and pleasure.

DEL. My child, I have all the comforts I deserve and desire, and find ample pleasure in my business.

RUTH. But, father, while you are almost prodigal with me, yet you do deny yourself very many things you really need and ought to have. It makes me feel both guilty and unhappy.

DEL. That's silly, child. The money spent on you by right belongs to you. It was your dear mother's portion, and you inherit it.

RUTH. But, Father, people say that you are enormously wealthy.

DEL. A great mistake, my child; all that I have I merely hold in trust.

RUTH. May I ask for whom?

DEL. One who will see me amply rewarded, in his good time, my child.

RUTH. But why not use some of my money? Take every dollar of it, and I will add the interest of a kiss to every dollar.

DEL. No, no, you little spendthrift. But if I really need it, I promise to call on you.

(Enter NANNY, with a skimmer in her hand.)

NAN. Miss Ruth, there's somethin' with a piece of glass with a string tied to it stuck in its eye, and suckin' a stick wants to see you. There's its ticket. (Hands her a card.)

RUTH. Lord De Puttipayte! Show him in. (Exit NANNY.)

DEL. And who is lord De Puttipayte?

RUTH. Only a titled fool, as you will soon discover. I met him at Mrs. Boodlebangs, and he has called a number of times since.

DEL. Ah! Fools, child, are sometimes the most dangerous.

RUTH. Nonsense, father.

(Enter LORD DE PUTTIPAYTE and NANNY.)

NAN. (Aside.) Lor', I hope he aint the one! (Exit NANNY.)

DEP. Awfully glad to see you, I assure you, Miss—Miss—Aw, Miss Delblot.

RUTH. My father, lord De Puttipayte.

DEP. Aw! How are you, old chappy?

DEL. Overwhelmed by this unexpected honor, I assure you.

DEP. Don't mention it. No, thanks. They bore me.

DEL. I must reluctantly leave the pleasure of entertaining your lordship to my daughter. I have important matters to attend to.

DEP. That's wight, my good fellow; look after the shop. See you later.

DEL. (Aside.) Even a title with such a thing as that attached to it, would disgust a less sensible girl than Ruth. He is perfectly harmless. (Exit DELMONT.)

RUTH. Won't you sit down, my lord?

DEP. (Aside.) This is deucedly awkward! What a dweadful oversight! I've got on my walking twowsers. (Aloud.) Thanks. (Sits down with great difficulty.) (Aside.) How aristocratically cool she is. By jove, she looks like a marble duchess, and could outfreeze the haughtiest of them, too, if she'd a mind to. And the colder she seems, the hotter I grow. Certain acceptance, lovely creature, rich father, social sensation, romantic return, ornament to ancestral halls. I flatter myself that I am a man of action, and, demme, if I don't go it! (Aloud.) Aw! Miss—Miss—Aw! Delrot; have you ever visited the mother country?

RUTH. No, my lord; but I should very much like to.

DEP. Would you, weally? Then, as the song says: "Come fly with me, o'er the moonlit sea."

RUTH. But how can you fly? You have no feathers, you know.

DEP. But I have golden wings, my dear Miss—Aw!—Miss Belmont, and I would gather you under them, as the devoted hen does her last spring chicken, you know.

RUTH. I fear that I am too much of a chicken to be able to follow you in such poetic flights, Lord DePuttipayte.

DEP. (Aside.) How cleverly she is leading me on. (Aloud.) My dear Miss—Aw!—Miss Delfrock, it may seem almost incwedible, but do you know that I started out to hook you, and, by jove, you've hooked me, instead.

RUTH. Hooked you, my lord? Surely you would not accuse me of putting you in a calf-skin binding?

DEP. No! not that kind of booking; but the kind of booking that means hooking, you know.

RUTH. But I don't know.

DEP. My dear Miss Aw!—Miss—Delfont, there are times in every great and distinguished man's career, when he feels irresistibly impelled to make hewoic self-sacwifices. That hour has come, and the man is here.

RUTH. My lord, pardon my native stupidity, but I am utterly at a loss to know what you are talking about.

DEP. Now, my dear Miss—Aw! Miss Delfront, pray don't get excited.

RUTH. That I am mystified, I must admit, but I never felt more tranquil, I assure you.

DEP. (Aside.) Well, by jove, I have. (Aloud.) That's wight, for the time has come when you will need all your self-possession to keep you from being deliriously dwowned in an unexpected flood of happiness and triumph.

RUTH. And not a life-preserver in sight! What shall I do?

DEP. Hear me, Miss, Aw! Miss—Denlot. I adore, I worship, I idolize; in fact, I love you dear Boaz—No! I mean Ruth. I would make a weal lady of you, and (Kneeling before her) here I lay my heart and title at your wavishing little tootsy-wootsies.

RUTH. What does all this trifling mean? Some one is coming! For heaven's sake get up, my lord!

(Enter FAIRLOOK, followed by NANNY, carrying a pillow, as RUTH drops her handkerchief for LORD DEP. to pick up.)

NANNY. (Aside.) This swipes the tabloo in the noble villain, and all three's got 'em. (Exit NANNY, hugging the pillow.)

DEP. (Aside.) The devil!

FAIR. (Picking up the handkerchief.) Allow me, Miss Delmont.

DEP. (Getting up with difficulty.) And while the wetch was in that position, I fired.

RUTH. And missed, my lord. Next time you should aim higher.

DEP. Y-a-a-s. That's good advice, and I'll twy and remember it.

RUTH. Thank you, my lord.

DEP. How are you, Mr. Fairday?

FAIR. Sir! My name is not Fairday, and you have the advantage of me.

RUTH. (Aside.) And that piece of rudeness is meant for me, sir.

DEP. Weally, have I? Then I'll try and keep it, (Aside) for I feel as though I'd lost everything else. (Aloud.) But I had forgotten. I promised to give Apebull a lesson in cane carrying, and attitude on the promenade. So, weally, I shall have to take my leave. Good day, Miss—Aw! Miss Demplot.

RUTH. Adieu, my lord.

DEP. (Aside.) A lord tossed overboard like a mouldy biscuit! It's incwedible. What would they say at the Lotus? If it gets out I'm ruined! I'll take the first steamer for England. (Exit LORD DEPUTTIPAYTE.)

FAIR. (Aside.) He can't cover his tracks with a halting lie like that. He was proposing to her. A lord is a dangerous rival with a lady, at any time. If murderously inclined jealousy be a sign of it, speculative purposes barred, for a professional woman hater, I'm badly scotched. Brazencraft, you stand in great danger of losing the trick. You must lead trumps.

RUTH. You are so silent, and frown so fiercely, Mr. Fairlook, you make me fear I have in some way unconsciously offended you.

FAIR. Yes!—That is, no! Not at all. I was merely trying to frame an acceptable excuse for my ill-mannered, and, I fear, most unwelcome intrusion. That stupid servant led me into it.

RUTH. Is that all? Then I freely pardon you. There was no harm done, I assure you.

FAIR. (Aside.) No harm done? That's a broad hint she has accepted him. (Aloud.) At least you shall not accuse me of tardiness in offering my congratulations.

RUTH. Congratulations! For what, pray?

FAIR. For what I unhappily saw.

RUTH. (Aside.) Now, were it not for his established reputation, I might flatter myself he was just a trifle jealous.

FAIR. (Aside.) She hesitates. I've lost the game!

RUTH. Is the spectacle of an idiot at a lady's feet so rare a one. Mr. Fairlook, that I am to be specially congratulated by a man of sense thereupon?

FAIR. Not generally; but if to it is added the attractions of a title, a great deal depends on what he was saying and doing there.

RUTH. I should scarcely have expected such an ungenerous and unkind innuendo from you, Mr. Fairlook. What Lord DePuttipayte was doing and saying is his secret, and you should respect it, as I do, if only from respect for me.

FAIR. Forgive me, Miss Delmont, for, indeed, I do respect you far too highly to displease you, or attempt to force myself upon your confidence. But I, to, have a secret, which this incident forces from me.

RUTH. (Aside.) How strangely my heart beats! What can he mean?

FAIR. I came to see your father.

RUTH. Well, I'm sure that's no very weighty secret, or compliment, either.

FAIR. Yes; the sincerest of compliments to you, and even more. I came to ask him for your hand; that is if your heart went with it. I did not intend that you should know this, but after what has passed, if your hand is pledged to another, may I not, with honor, beseech you not to uselessly subject me to the humiliation of a refusal?

RUTH. (Aside.) He loves me, and is worthy of my love. (Aloud.) Your candor compels me to sacrifice modest scruples to the truth. My hand, as yet, is free.

FAIR. And your heart?

RUTH. It is hardly generous to press me quite so closely.

FAIR. If I appear unreasonable, it is because all my hopes of happiness hang on your answer. You have heard that I have been as ice to all your sex, and it was true.

RUTH. (Aside.) And I am most truly glad to hear it.

FAIR. I never knew I had a heart until I learned so from your eyes. It lay cold; dead; irresponsive to every wile and fascination, until the witchery of your beauty called it into glorious life, and melted it as melts an April frost. Dear Ruth, I love you; and who can measure or define the all-o'ermastering strength and sincerity of a first and only love, that has the power to thus transform me?

RUTH. (Aside.) Measured by what it has awakened here, it seems but weak and transient.

FAIR. You are silent.

RUTH. (Aside.) Yes; eloquently silent, from commingled joy and doubt.

FAIR. Is it from sympathy and sweet compliance; or from cold indifference? Answer me, Ruth, and frankly. I implore you, answer me!

RUTH. O, sir, I scarcely know how to answer you, and yet, perhaps, I am not entirely indifferent to your avowal.

FAIR. Must I base all my fond hopes of gaining your affections on such a dubious concession as that?

RUTH. No! Why should love, purity and truth in woman, more than man, conceal themselves behind coquettish arts; counterfeit fashionable shamefacedness, and only seem to hesitate to match their fellows? I love you, John, and have done so from the first.

FAIR. My darling! My infinitely generous darling! A whole life's most faithful devotion shall reward your priceless gift and noble candor.

RUTH. Heaven grant it, John! Natures like mine give all, and they demand as much. Should you deceive me, I could not forgive it. Should you prove false, it would surely kill me.

FAIR. Then shall you be immortal, as are the other angels.

RUTH. You, and you only, have the power to make my love as immortal as theirs. But, alas, we are as blind as love, and as unreckoning as children. What will my father say?

FAIR. Leave that to me.

RUTH. But he will never consent to my marrying a Christian.

FAIR. I will convince him that I am one in faith, as I am one in heart and spirit with you, sweet saint.

RUTH. When will you see him, love?

FAIR. Let me plunge in at once and cross this Hellespont.

RUTH. But if you fail, I fear that I shall sink with you.

FAIR. Fear not; I am no weak Leander; and with such a Hero waiting for me, I cannot fail.

RUTH. Hark! I hear my father's voice. What shall we do?

FAIR. Leave me to meet him. Where cowards, through faltering fail, courage compels success.

RUTH. Heaven grant it!

FAIR. Amen! (Exit RUTH.)
She is mine! mine! And false, mercenary and all-unworthy of her as I am, it makes me madly happy.

(Enter DELMONT.)

DEL. (Stopping at the door.) There's half a dollar missing, and although I've wasted five dollars' worth of time on it, I can't account for it. Nanny! Nanny, I say!

NAN. (Outside.) Yes, sir.

DEL. Have you seen anything of a stray fifty cent piece?

NAN. Lor', sir, no! I don't believe I'd even know one if I seed it.

DEL. I'll wager that you would if you could have it for the finding. (Enters room and sees Fairlook.) Mr. Fairlook, I believe?

FAIR. Yes, Mr. Delmont, I was waiting to see you.

14

DEL. I hope I have not detained you, sir.

FAIR. Not at all. My thoughts have been pleasant company during the brief time I have waited.

DEL. Few men can say as much. What is the nature of your business, may I ask?

FAIR. Both delicate and important, sir; and one that should be dealt with in a manly and straightforward manner. Frankly, then, sir, I most earnestly and respectfully ask your permission to address your daughter.

DEL. For what purpose?

FAIR. That of marriage.

DEL. Marriage? You marry my daughter?

FAIR. If I have your permission and her favor, sir.

DEL. Does my daughter know aught of this, sir?

FAIR. Upon my honor, nothing.

DEL. You are sure of that?

FAIR. I have said it, sir.

DEL. (Aside.) But I don't believe it. (Aloud.) I would not seem abrupt, Mr. Fairlook, but your example compels me to say frankly that what you ask it is impossible to grant.

FAIR. But, Mr. Delmont. I am a man of good standing and habits, and, as these papers will satisfy you, able to support a wife in something more than comfort. (Aside.) And I will trust them to hoodwink even your sharp eyes. (Tenders papers to Delmont.)

DEL. I do not care to see them, sir. Strange as it may appear to you, in this instance, money is but a secondary consideration with me.

FAIR. I respect the sentiment. But, surely, Mr. Delmont, you know nothing against me?

DEL. I know nothing in your favor, sir, and in an affair of this kind, that is very much against you. Excuse me for dealing with you in a manly and straightforward manner, for I am a father, and the circumstances demand it. I know that you are a fashionable idler. My daughter's happiness is very dear to me, and I cannot intrust it to one of that class.

FAIR. But, pray consider, Mr. Delmont, that I have had no incentive to be otherwise.

DEL. Is there, then, no good to be done in this world, Mr. Fairlook?

FAIR. Assuredly; and a great deal. Give me your daughter and she shall teach me how to do it.

DEL. The risk is far too great to justify the experiment. I fear, sir, the lesson would come altogether too late in your life to be of any service. Besides, you seem to forget, sir, that I am a Jew. You are not of my faith, and that alone would constitute an insurmountable objection.

FAIR. As a proof of my sincerity, I am prepared to renounce Christianity this very day, and embrace your religion. I swear it!

DEL. What! And thus make sudden apostacy pander to hot-footed desire?

FAIR. From any other man, sir, except Ruth Delmont's Father, I would resent such a charge as that as a deadly insult. But I can pardon even that in you. As you are so evidently pre-determined to misunderstand me, it would be utterly useless to prolong this painful interview.

DEL. Utterly.

FAIR. Good day, Mr. Delmont. The time will come when you will learn to know me better.

DEL. (Aside.) I hardly think it. (Aloud.) Stay, sir. (Rings the bell.)

(Enter NANNY.)

Send my daughter to me at once.

NAN. (Aside.) The noble villian's run agin the stony-hearted parient, and the whirligig bridge will be painted red with ge-ar. (Exit NANNY.)

FAIR. But, Mr. Delmont, it is entirely unnecessary that Miss Ruth should be summoned.

DEL. I have no family secrets from my daughter, sir.

FAIR. (Aside.) I hope she'll look sharp for danger signals.

(Enter RUTH.)

RUTH. (Aside.) My heart prophesied but too truly. Alas, he has failed! (Aloud.) Did you wish to see me, father?

DEL. Yes, my child. Are you acquainted with this gentleman?

RUTH. Mr. Fairlook? I have met him quite frequently.

DEL. Then you must know him well.

RUTH. Yes, father—that is, quite well.

DEL. He has done us the honor of asking your hand in marriage, and I have declined it. Absolutely, irrevocably declined it. Do you understand me, my child?

RUTH. Yes, father.

DEL. Now you may go, sir.

[CURTAIN.]

ACT IV.

SCENE 1.—A STREET.

(*Enter* NIGHTHAWK *from right and* FAIRLOOK *from left.*)

NIGHT. Halloo, Fairlook! What news? How goes the foray into rich Judea?

FAIR. She loves me.

NIGHT. You are a lucky dog.

FAIR. I feel more like a mangy cur, and could curse myself that she does love me.

NIGHT. Well, here is a go! What an unreasonable, spoilt child it is, to be sure. Squalling and bumping its own head, and all because it has got just what it cried for.

FAIR. Cold and callous as I am. I've got more than I bargained for—a lesson in unselfish love and confiding purity that has well-nigh conquered me.

NIGHT. "'Tis said, that even a lion will flee, from a maid in the strength of her purity;" but I did not think you that kind of a beast.

FAIR. What does the lion care what the jackal thinks? Why did you tempt me into this infernal scheme?

NIGHT. For good and substantial reasons already stated. But I miscalculated with whom I had to deal. The girl's a witch.

FAIR. She is an angel, and, in all noble attributes, as far above us as is the Seventh Heaven above the lowest depths of Hell.

NIGHT. (*Aside.*) I must give this hooked shark line or he'll swamp everything. (*Aloud.*) Give her up, then.

FAIR. I've tried a thousand times harder to do so than I ever did to commit a crime, and failed.

NIGHT. Why so?

FAIR. Because I love her so I cannot do it.

NIGHT. Then marry her.

FAIR. Her father rejected me with galling disdain and bitter insults, and even called her in to witness it.

NIGHT. Which goes to prove the wisdom of my first advice. He has stripped himself of all right to consideration. Besides, Fairlook, and mark well what I say, such a girl as that loves but once. If you really love her, you cannot abandon her. It would kill her. You have no choice. You *must* marry her.

FAIR. I never looked at it in that light.

NIGHT. It don't require a second look to prove that I am right. Besides, I am reliably advised that Miss Delmont inherits quite a fortune from her mother, which makes her largely independent of her father.

FAIR. So, the sneaking jackal would have me play the lion and marry her, that I may rob her to pay him.

NIGHT. The nobler beast would be ashamed to make such a return as that for good advice. I never thought of it. I'm entirely willing to trust the future and your word for my recompense. (*Aside.*) And I'll make you pay cent. per cent. usury for every cut you've given me.

FAIR. That sounds fair enough, and if I've hastily done you injustice, I regret it.

NIGHT. Say no more about it; it is forgotten already. I'm prepared to make all allowances for the unreasonableness of love, and especially in such a victim. But, seriously, Fairlook, I'm getting dead sick of this sort of life. I don't pretend to put it on high moral grounds. It's too devilish dangerous and precarious. So, to the rest of my good advice, I'll add this best piece of all: marry the girl; make her a good husband; reform, and I'll follow suit.

FAIR. Now I begin to believe that Ruth is an angelic witch. Do you really mean it?

NIGHT. Upon my life, I do.

FAIR. Then, Brace Nighthawk, for the first time in my life I respect you. Shake! It's a bargain.

NIGHT. (*Aside.*) And one that will be broken on both sides. (*Aloud.*) Well, then, let's go and pay a brimming libation to the fair goddess of good resolutions.

FAIR. Aye! And drown what we have been ten thousand fathoms deep.

(*Exit all.*)

16

SCENE 2.—A SECLUDED NOOK IN CENTRAL PARK.

(*Enter* RUTH DELMONT.)

RUTH. Why is it that our wayward hearts ever most desire the things denied them, and crave most for most forbidden fruits? How rapturously delicious are these stolen interviews. My heart would starve without them. Why should my father, for the first time, so play the hateful tyrant with me, and in the very thing, too, where my happiness is most concerned? Why should he so cruelly interfere in an affair that is so entirely mine? No one asks him to marry John, I'm sure. Then why should he object to him, and when he offers to become a convert to our faith, too? I'm sure that's very complimentary to me; and he is fit to be a prince, or a high priest in Israel. Why don't he come? What keeps him? It seems as though I had already waited an age for him.

(*Enter* FAIRLOOK. *He steals up behind Ruth and kisses her.*)

RUTH. Sir! Why, John! How you frightened me. You ought to be ashamed of yourself. I never knew you were a thief, before.

FAIR. Because I stole a kiss? Your loveliness is far the guiltier accomplice for having tempted me beyond endurance. But, in proof of my penitence, I will return it.

RUTH. You shall not thus cheaply bribe your judge until you clear yourself of a more serious crime. You are beginning early, sir, to play the tardy wooer.

FAIR. Sweet judge, I am but a half-a-minute late.

RUTH. Fie, then, upon you for a halting laggard. You should have been a full half-hour too soon; carving my name in circling hearts upon the trees; composing love-lorn sonnets to my eyes, and playing the sighing and impatient Orlando. But I'll be generous and forgive you, if you'll but tell me again, and yet again, that you love me, and are happy in my love.

FAIR. My Rosebud, I could not half tell you in a whole millenium's length how much I love you.

RUTH. That's very long, and yet but half an answer.

FAIR. Was Adam happy outside of Paradise?

RUTH. I'm sure he should have been. He had Eve with him.

FAIR. Yes, and with her all the best of Paradise; but I have no such dear companion to cheer my lonely and despondent hours with sympathy and love.

RUTH. Dear John, you have me. Pray is not that enough?

FAIR. It would be more than enough to make the earth a paradise to me. Ruth, do you really love me as much as you say?

RUTH. Heaven knows my heart, I do!

FAIR. Are you prepared to give me proof of it?

RUTH. Have I not already done so, dearest?

FAIR. Yes, and no.

RUTH. What more could you rightly ask of me?

FAIR. But one thing.

RUTH. And what is that?

FAIR. Your fullest confidence.

RUTH. But, John, you have that, too.

FAIR. Are you sure?

RUTH. As sure as that I love you.

FAIR. Then marry me.

RUTH. Alas. I cannot, without my father's consent.

FAIR. And that you will never gain until you do.

RUTH. Oh, have pity and patience, darling! Bye-and-bye he may relent.

FAIR. Never, until we boldly force him to it. Beneath the weary shadows of that dim and distant bye-and-bye we may grow old and die in waiting. Be reasonable, Ruth. We can conceal our marriage until a favorable opportunity occurs to disclose it. Your father will then see that further opposition is worse than useless, and make the best of it. He loves you too much to do otherwise.

RUTH. John, I would gladly die for you, but this I must refuse you.

FAIR. Then you do not love and trust me as you say.

RUTH. How can you be so cruel and unjust?

FAIR. It is you, who are cruel, and I that would be kind. Things cannot go on in this way, Ruth. Your father is likely to discover our secret at any moment, and then we shall be hopelessly parted. The time has come when you must choose between us.

RUTH. Alas, I have no choice!

FAIR. Then, in mercy to us both, and most to you, far well, my first and only love—farewell, forever! (*Going.*)

RUTH. Oh, Heavenly Father, guide and sustain me! My heart is breaking. Farewell, John! No! No! I cannot give him up! O, John! My king! My more than husband; come back to me! (*Fairlook returns to her.*) Whither thou goest, I will go! Thy people shall be my people, and thy God, my God!

FAIR. And, life of my soul, I will be one with you!

SCENE 3—A STREET.

(*Enter ALICE, crying.*)

ALICE You horrid, cruel, ungentleman, little forty thieves, you! You'r badder than the baddest boy in the Sunday-school book. (*A voice outside—"Rats!"*) Maybe the rats will eat you up; just like they did that wicked old bishop in his big stone castle.

(*Enter DELMONT.*)

DEL. What's the matter, my little maiden, all forlorn?

ALICE. A juvalrine depravity snatched my pennies, that I was going to get some bread with, and, Oh, dear, Mamma and me's so hungry!

DEL. The heartless young scoundrel! But, never mind, here's a famous remedy for drying up the tears of honest poverty, and I would that more of it was wisely used for that purpose. (*Hands her money.*)

ALICE. O, thank you, sir! Aren't you one of those angels the good book tells about, that hides their wings and goes around wearing men's clothes?

DEL. Far from it, my child.

ALICE. Why, I know now who you are! You are the Mr. Goodman I helped Mamma to pray for.

DEL. What's that? Why, bless my soul, it's widow Arthur's little girl! What are you doing here?

ALICE. Our pretty cottage burnded all up, and Mamma was dreadfully burnded, too, saving me. If she hadn't, she'd lost everything. We's most starved to death ever since.

DEL. Why did she not let me know of this?

ALICE. That's what I tolded her, but she said she could not bear to pay any more taxes on your bounty, and that God would take care of us; but, though we've both prayed, O, so hard, he never comes. Perhaps, Mr. Goodman, he's so old that he's deaf and can't see or hear us.

DEL. He has heard you, my poor child. Where is your mother?

ALICE. Down in the dark alley and up ever so many stairs.

DEL. Come, we'll go to her at once.

ALICE. Yes, Mr. Goodman; but please don't walk very fast. My legs seem so heavy lately.

DEL. Poor little thing! Then I'll make mine do duty for both. (*Taking her up in his arms.*) So, here we go!

ALICE. This is the way. You play good genie and I'll be the bootiful princess of Chinaware, and we'll fly away to the bakery.

(*Enter FAIRLOOK and NIGHTHAWK—the former intoxicated.*)

FAIR. (*To Delmont.*) Halloo, old baby carriage!

ALICE. You has a bigger load than he has, Mr. Whiskey Carriage!

DEL. Hush, child! They are beneath notice.

(*Exit DELMONT and ALICE.*)

NIGHT. Are you blind? That was Delmont.

FAIR. No! Was it? It's a smart man that knows his own father-in-law; but a smarter one that knows his own son-in-law.' I'll drop 'round, apologize, introduce myself, and ask him to take a drink.

NIGHT. You'll do nothing of the sort.

FAIR. Won't I! Well, you try to stop me, and you won't do any calling, except for arnica, for some time to come.

NIGHT. I never saw you in this shape before. You're crazy!

FAIR. You're drunk. Go to bed.

NIGHT. You're going to the devil.

FAIR. No, he's following me.

(*Exit FAIRLOOK followed by NIGHTHAWK.*)

SCENE 4.—RECEPTION ROOM IN DELMONT'S HOUSE.

(Enter NANNY with broom and dustpan followed by FAIRLOOK.)

NANNY. *(After Fairlook has made a maudlin effort to take hold of her and she has pushed him away.)* Hands off the brasses. *(Aside.)* The noble villian's as boozy as a Bosting prize-fighter.

FAIR. *(Throwing a handful of change at her.)* Take that to polish them up with.

NAN. *(Sweeping up the coins.)* They're what dad used to call shiners, and I'm not too proud to try 'em.

FAIR. Where's my—I mean Miss Ruth?

NAN. I don't know, sir.

FAIR. *(Falling into a chair.)* Then I'll wait for her.

NAN. Take a friend's advice, Mr. Fairlook, and don't do it.

FAIR. That was Punch's advice to a man about to get married. It don't apply to me.

NAN. Yes it do, Mr. Fairlook.

FAIR. How so?

NAN. Because she'll never be Mrs. Fairlook if she sees you in this shape.

FAIR. Won't she? I'll just bet you ten to one she does. What's the matter with my shape anyway?

(Ruth, speaking from outside—Nanny! Nanny!)

NANNY. Holy smoke, there she is now! And I'll just bet you a hundred to ten you'll think the noble villian fell into the cistern hisself, in January, and wished he'd a drownded there.

(Ruth, outside—Nanny, where are you?)

NAN. Yes, mum, I's comin'.   *(Exit NANNY.)*

(Enter RUTH.)

RUTH. John here, and not well? What can Nanny mean? *(Sees Fairlook dozing in a chair.)* John, my love, what is the matter? Are you ill? For pity's sake, answer me!

FAIR. Yes: terrible pain in my brandy and peppermint—took too much colic—gone to head.

RUTH. His mind wanders! He is delirious! John, can't you understand me, darling? What brought you here?

FAIR. A hack. Is that you, lady-bird? Come perch on my knee, and I'll sing to thee.

RUTH. This is dreadful! What shall I do? What shall I do?

FAIR. *(Staggering to his feet.)* Stand steady, lady-bird. *(Embraces her.)*

RUTH. *(Breaking away from him.)* Merciful heavens, he's drunk! *(Fairlook approaches her.)* Stand back, sir! There's pollution in your touch!

FAIR. Won't you kiss and make up?

RUTH. Never, sir, until you beg my pardon on your knees, and swear never to let me see you thus degraded again. Oh, John, my husband, is this your love for me? If so, then strike me dead, before I learn to hate and despise you.

FAIR. First time in my life, I swear it. Must have been drugged. Forgive me, darling, and I'll do anything you say.

RUTH. Then, if you have any love and pity for me, take mercy on me, and leave this place at once. Every moment you remain is an age of agony to me.

FAIR. Give me just one forgiving kiss and I'll do it.

RUTH. Only obey me and I'll give you anything. *(Kisses him.)* Now go, John, that's a dear, good fellow! Go instantly, and while there is yet time.

FAIR. But when shall I see you again, sweetheart?

RUTH. This evening! To-morrow! Any time! But now, Go! Go!

FAIR. I'll go as fast as John Gilpin did, and as reluctantly. *(Going.)*

(Enter DELMONT and DR. STERNLAW.)

When we meet again *(runs against Delmont)*—What do you mean?

RUTH. *(Aside.)* My father! What will become of us?

DEL. You here?

FAIR. So it would seem.

DEL. I did not expect to meet you a second time to-day.

FAIR. And I hardly expected to run against you again, either.

DEL. How dare you cross my threshold and intrude upon my daughter? Your very presence breeds debauchery and contamination.

FAIR. Opinions may differ about that. Ask her.

DEL. Ruth, what does this mean? Have you received this besotted reprobate, and in this condition?

RUTH. I could not avoid it, father.

DEL. I beg your pardon for asking such a question. Of course you could not help it. The drunken blackguard forced himself upon you. (To Fairlook.) Quit the house before I so far forget myself as to soil my hands with you.

FAIR. (Advancing.) Would you?

DEL. (Advancing.) Would I?

RUTH. (Rushing between them.) Father! Father! What would you do?

DEL. Stand aside!

RUTH. Not if you kill me will I permit you two to rend each other. Force is not required. He will go—he promised me. Won't you, Mr. Fairlook? I implore you. (Aside.) If you would not murder me, go!

DEL. Peace, child! You shall not demean yourself by pleading with, or even speaking to, such as he. But, as you wish it, there shall be no violence. We will dispose of him more fittingly. (Ringing the bell.)

FAIR. Look you, Delmont; on that girl's account, I've stood more from you than I ever did from any other living man. I'll take no more of it.

(Enter NANNY.)

DEL. (To Nanny.) Summon an officer at once.

NAN. An hossifer?

DEL. Do as I bid you, instantly.

NAN. (Aside.) Well, if I calls a cop may I be pinched fust.

(Exit NANNY.)

(To Fairlook.) I'll teach you the only kind of lesson that such as you can understand, and put you beyond the power of insulting either of us further.

RUTH. Father, though I disobey you, this must not be. (To Fairlook.) Leave us, sir, I command you! To stay means ruin! Are you mad?

FAIR. Yes, baited to it. (To Delmont.) You'll send me to the lock-up, will you? Well, then, you'll send my wife to keep me company.

DEL. That's no affair of mine. It would seem a fitting place for any woman that would call you husband.

FAIR. Would it, indeed? Well, then, come Ruth, we'd best be moving.

RUTH. (Aside.) Lost! Lost!

DEL. (Seizing a chair.) Dare to so much as even look at her again, and I'll brain you.

FAIR. I don't ask even your permission to address my own wife.

DEL. My daughter your wife! Ha, ha! Why this is the monstrous grotesqueness of delirium tremens.

FAIR. Does she look as though it was?

DEL. Ruth, why do you hang your head and tremble so? Fear not, my daughter. Face this foul slanderer; tell him he lies, and trust me to avenge it.

RUTH. I cannot, father.

DEL. Cannot? But I see, poor child, this scene has unnerved you. Collect your senses and answer me.

RUTH. I have already done so, father.

DEL. You have not answered me, but shall! What is this man to you?

RUTH. All that he claims, father.

DEL. I'll not believe my loins could breed such wanton, hideous treachery and ingratitude. The insanity of fear has made you, for the first time, stain your virgin lips with falsehood.

RUTH. Father, I cannot add the weight of falsehood to my other sins. He speaks the truth.

DEL. And you, my only child, that I have loved and trusted so utterly, live to cower there and tell me that you have forsaken and betrayed your God, your people, and your father, for such a drunken scoundrel and fortune-hunter as that?

RUTH. Oh, father, on my soul you wrong him! He is brave, true and generous, and I love him. Forgive him for my sake.

DEL. I will forgive him before I will forgive such shameless treason in my own flesh and blood. I am not his father. You! you! make me thank God that your mother did not live to this day. Who are you, that you should ask forgiveness? Away with you! I know you not! I had a daughter once, but she is dead, too.

FAIR. Take her back, sir, and, much as I love her, I swear to you never to look upon her face again.

DEL. I will not be outdone in generosity: not even by a thief. Keep her, and may her poverty not lessen her attractions. When you stole her from me,

20

you robbed her of even what her mother left her; for if she married without my full consent, she lost all. Such a price as that should purchase a rare husband.

RUTH. Father, pardon! pardon! For my dear, dead mother's sake do not completely crush the heart of her poor child.

FAIR. Are you a hell-born tiger, that you refuse to hear her?

DEL. I hear the snarling of the sneaking wolf that devoured my one poor ewe lamb—nothing more.

RUTH. (*Kneeling to Dr. Sternlaw.*) Rabbi, Rabbi! I have always loved and honored you, and I implore you to intercede for me. Speak to him! Oh, reason with him! He will listen to you.

RAB. I am powerless. You have voluntarily placed yourself beyond the pale of my protection.

RUTH. Is there, then, no mercy in Heaven, or on Earth, for me?

RAB. You have said it.

FAIR. And I say, you hoary-headed, heartless bigot, that you are more devil than priest. Come away, Ruth, or I shall do mischief here. (*Takes Ruth by the hand.*)

RUTH. Father, may I not say farewell to you?

DEL. I disown, disinherit and forget you. Begone, before I curse you, even as I do him.

RUTH. No, no, father! Not that! Not that!

DEL. Away with you! Away with you! (*Ruth and Fairlook go out.*) God of my fathers, why hast thou forsaken me? (*Falls into a chair, with his face buried in his arms.*)

[CURTAIN.]

ACT V.

SCENE I.—FAIRLOOK'S LODGINGS.

(Enter FAIRLOOK.)

FAIR. What has come over me? My wits, courage, and even luck, fail me; and at the time, too, when I need them most. Her purity and loving trust seem to have exercised my twin familiar devils of swindling art and never-failing nerve, and irresolution and weak remorse have usurped their place, to render every plan and effort dangerously futile. Is there no master-stroke by which I can secure the means to leave this place, and in some strange land begin a new life, worthy of such a wife? Satan, my patron saint, smile on me but once again, and I vow never more to importune you. Surely my devotion to you deserves this much. *(Knock at door.)* Another vainly climbing creditor, most likely. Come in!

(Enter NIGHTHAWK.)

NIGHT. Good morning, Fairlook.

FAIR. Well met. I was just thinking of you.

NIGHT. Pleasant thoughts, I trust.

FAIR. At least appropriate ones.

NIGHT. Where is your wife?

FAIR. Out for a mouthful of fresh air. It is one luxury she can enjoy, poor girl, because it costs her nothing.

NIGHT. That's lucky, for I want some private talk with you. But what ails you? You look as chop-fallen as a homeless dog.

FAIR. I am one.

NIGHT. Well, it must be from choice, then.

FAIR. From choice, you limb of hell? Do you think I'd see her want, from choice? I'd coin my black heart's blood, drop by drop, to purchase comfort for her.

NIGHT. There is a way much easier, and far less heroic.

FAIR. Don't trifle with me. I'm desperate, and wont stand it.

NIGHT. I am not trifling, and deliberately repeat, there is an easier way.

FAIR. How, then?

NIGHT. You have but to stretch out your hand and take what justly belongs to her.

FAIR. A fool's advice. The law wont let me touch it.

NIGHT. Then do it without the law.

FAIR. That is impossible.

NIGHT. Again I say it is an easy thing, if you can but summon up the pluck to undertake it.

FAIR. If you dare to slur my courage, I'll give you ample proof of it.

NIGHT. I need none; but this is a peculiar case. Be reasonable, can't you, and hear me out?

FAIR. If you don't want me to shake it out of you, come to the point at once.

NIGHT. Delmont keeps large sums of money in his house, besides valuable securities, which, with the backing of your magic pen, might be readily negotiated.

FAIR. He would even see his daughter starve before he would give us a farthing; and I would rather do so than beg one from him.

NIGHT. Precisely! But supposing we were to call, very privately, rather late, some convenient evening, and kindly save him the trouble of refusing?

FAIR. What! Would you tempt me to rob my own wife's father?

NIGHT. By no means! For, in the first place, he is not her father. He has disowned her, and you know him well enough to understand that he will never forgive her: at least, not so long as you live. Secondly, and morally, there is no robbery in this case. You are merely taking what rightfully belongs to your wife, and of which he would rob her, on a mere legal quibble.

FAIR. That's true; curse his heartless avarice! But while these arguments justify me, they don't apply to you.

NIGHT. O, I'm merely helping you to your own, you see.

FAIR. Verily, a model and most disinterested friend.

NIGHT. Not entirely, and I make no pretense of being. The fact is, I'm as hard pushed as yourself, and this city is getting too hot to hold me. I must have money; I'm willing to take the risk of helping you to get it, and I expect you to pay me well for it. Now we understand each other, and I've but one more argument to add, and it's a mighty strong one, you will do well to weigh. You've bungled lately, and gossip's tongue is whispering some rather ugly things about you. Soon she will be in full cry, snarling and snapping at your heels. Consider what that means;—exposure, ruin and disgrace. And what will your wife think of you?

FAIR. Say no more! I'll do it! But, in her holy name, I swear that it shall be the last crime of my life.

NIGHT. And of mine. I'd best be going now. Meet me at the Club in an hour, and we'll perfect our plans. You'll not fail me?

FAIR. When did you ever know me fail to keep an appointment with the devil?

(Enter RUTH.)

RUTH. O! John, dear, I've had such a delightful walk. That is, it would have been had you been with me. (To Nighthawk.) Excuse me, sir, I did not see you.

NIGHT. How do you do, Mrs. Fairlook? You certainly are the charming picture of perfect health.

RUTH. I am quite well, thank you, sir.

NIGHT. Delighted to hear it. Well, I must be off. So long, old fellow. See you later. Good day, Mrs. Fairlook.

RUTH. Good morning, sir. (Exit NIGHTHAWK.)

FAIR. (Aside.) She looks like an accusing angel.

RUTH. What did that man want here, John? He seems a bird of evil omen.

FAIR. Nonsense, my superstitious little pet. He merely called to advise me of a transaction that may greatly benefit the distinguished Fairlook family.

RUTH. I detest and fear him. Oh, my husband, trust to the instinct of the one that loves you best of all, and have nothing to do with that man.

FAIR. Not after to-day, fair sibyl. I swear to you; for then I hope to take you far from here, where naught but peace and happiness await you, for all the years to come.

RUTH. This seems a very sudden resolution.

FAIR. And yet, sweetheart, it is one I have long and seriously contemplated. But, if you object, I will abandon it at once.

RUTH. John, dear, do you remember what I said to you the day I consented to become your wife?

FAIR. Yes, darling.

RUTH. I meant it, John, and hold it sacred, as I do every promise made to you.

FAIR. Oh, my precious, peerless wife! Would to God that I were worthy of you!

RUTH. Hush, my darling! I will not permit even you to disparage my husband, lord and king. I am the one to plead unworthiness.

FAIR. No! no! Don't say that, Ruth! I could die with shame and remorse, when I think of what I have brought you to.

RUTH. That was an accident, love, born of a moment's weakness; for which you have amply atoned by the most tender penitence. It must have come sooner, or later, and let us hope that it is best as it is.

FAIR. Hereafter, if I can prevent it, you shall never have occasion for regret. Trust me that much, my life.

RUTH. I have trusted you with my love, life and honor, John. It was the only portion I could bring you. Treasure it; for if it ever grows valueless to you, in that hour I shall surely die.

FAIR. (Aside.) Oh, innocence; what boundless torture you can inflict on guilt! I can endure this no longer!

(Enter NANNY, with a basket.)

NAN. Can I come in?

RUTH. Why, it's Nanny! (Embracing her.) You dear, darling, blessed thing, you! How glad I am to see you!

NAN. Well, this is a unexpected honor; as the gentleman said when the hangman bowed to him.

FAIR. How do you do, Nanny? I'm right glad to see you, too.

NAN. Thank you kindly, sir.

RUTH. Come and sit right down here this minute, and let me feast my eyes on you.

NAN. I've fetched somethin' for you to feast your stummick on, and that's more substansholer. Thing-a-migigs I made myself, an' they's got a real home taste to 'em, too, Miss Ruth.

Ruth. How can I ever thank you?

Fair. This is evidently a case where two is company and three is none. So I'll leave you to yourselves. By-the-way, Ruth, I have to go to Norwalk on the business I spoke to you about, and may not return before morning. So don't sit up for me.

Ruth. You never staid away so long as that before.

Fair. Nor would I now, were I not making a great sacrifice for your sake, dearest. Don't make it harder by objecting so pitifully.

Ruth. If it is for the best, I'll bear it bravely, John. There (Kissing him), take that big kiss for good luck, and heaven speed you in your enterprise, and safely back to me.

Fair. (Aside.) A wish that seems to chill me like a curse.

(Exit FAIRLOOK.)

Nan. You look pale and thin, Miss Ruth. Is the noble villain kind to you?

Ruth. Who?

Nan. The noble villian. Him. (Pointing over her shoulder with her thumb.)

Ruth. Have no fears on that score. He is the best of husbands.

Nan. Well, he'd better be, if he don't want a taste of my quality; as the red pepper said to the monkey's eye.

Ruth. How is my father, Nanny?

Nan. Well, he ain't percatly in shape for a six days' go-as-you-please in Madison Square Garden; but he's so's to be able to look on.

Ruth. Poor father! Does he ever speak of me?

Nan. Never—that is, I mean before company, you know; but he do talk a great deal to hisself lately, and once, I realy berlieve, I actoaly caught him cryin'. (Ruth weeps.) (Aside.) Burn my fool kisser, what did I let that out for? Don't cry, Miss Ruth, or you'll set my pumps to goin', and they leaks orfully when they gits started. (Cries loudly.) Cheer up, that's a dear. I really berlieve he's weaknin'.

Ruth. Weakening?

Nan. Yes; he's softnin' wonderful, and, would you berlieve it? never finds no fault no more about anythin' I busts or spiles; and even seems to take comfort in seein' me around, like. I really and truly berlieves, on my most solemnest and sacredest swear, that his mulishness is gittin' winded, and that he'll throw up the sponge.

Ruth. Throw up the sponge?

Nan. You bet! And buy all the veal in the butcher shop, and hire a brass band, to welcome the proudengle gal home agin.

Ruth. Oh, Nanny, if I could but hope he would ever forgive me!

Nan. Never you fear, Miss Ruth. It's 'comin', and its got to come; 'cause its agin natur for it to do otherwise. So just dry your sweet eyes, and hang on to the sheet iron of hope. I'll stick to him, 'cause I promised you I would, and I'll watch his sympterms like a big-bug doctor would them of a railroad president.

Ruth. But I may have to leave here to-morrow, Nanny, and it seems as though I should die if I did not see his dear face once more, and it may be for the last time.

Nan. Lor', that's easier'n fallin' through the cellar door! Put on your things and come right along with me. He's orful res'less, and wanders round, and aint likely to come in 'till all hours in the mornin'. I'll slip you up to my boodwar in the attic, and you can get a good peep at him somehow.

Ruth. I must and will risk it. I cannot resist the impulse.

Nan. Let me just put this truck away, and trot's the word.

(Exit NANNY, with basket.)

Ruth. All my father's wealth could not buy one such friend as that.

(Enter NANNY.)

Nan. Now, come along. To hesitate is to be bilked.

(Exit all.)

SCENE II.—The Reception Room in Delmont's House.

(Enter DELMONT.)

Del. It is very late, and I am weak and weary, almost unto death, and yet, neither my once sovereign will, nor the most potent sense-benumbing drugs, can conquer or appease the pain and hunger ever gnawing here (placing his hand on his heart); or give me but one little hour of sleep. This place, but yesterday so

sunny with the radiance of her beauty, and softly tuneful with the melody of her
sweet voice, seems like a dark and silent living grave ; whose vacant coldness chills
me to the soul. (*Sits in easy chair at table, and looks at a document.*) This seals
and satisfies the law of my belief. The law ? Is there, then, no hope of an appeal
from it to the omnipotence of mercy and forgiveness, far above the limits of its
iron jurisdiction ? The pride of habit and of doctrine answer, No ! But outraged
nature, with outstretched arms and streaming eyes, sobs, Yes ; and like the royal
mourner, of whose lineage I am, and whose name I bear, my over-tortured heart
cries out : Oh, Ruth, my child ! my child ! Would to God that I had died for
thee ! (*Sinks back in chair.*)

(*Enter* FAIRLOOK *and* NIGHTHAWK, *roughly dressed and masked ; the latter carrying a bag of burglar's tools.*)

NIGHT. All's quiet, and the coast is clear. (*Advances ; sees Delmont ; starts
back ; takes Fairlook by the arm and points to Delmont.*)

FAIR. What's to be done ?

NIGHT. (*Producing a slung-shot.*) He's asleep. Let's make it a sound one.

FAIR. (*Seizing Nighthawk.*) Not that ; unless you want to die yourself. I will
not have her father's blood upon my hands. It is enough to gag and bind him.
(*Nighthawk takes off his neckerchief and steals toward Delmon . Looks at him
and stops.*)

NIGHT. Great God, Fairlook, he's dead !

FAIR. Dead ? Yes, so indeed he is. There's no mistaking the imprint of that
awful seal. Cover up his face. Those stony eyes seem to summon me to join him.

NIGHT. (*Covering Delmont's face with the neckerchief.*) Weak superstition.
He'll trouble you no more.

FAIR. Who knows that ?

NIGHT. (*Opening a bag and laying a jimmy and one or two other tools on the
table.*) At least he'll not meddle with the job we have in hand, and I'd thank him
for his consideration, if he could hear me.

FAIR. What is that paper in his hand ?

NIGHT. We have no time to waste in idle curiosity.

FAIR. Give it to me, I say !

NIGHT. (*Takes paper and looks at it.*) And well it may interest you. It is his
will. (*Hands paper to Fairlook.*)

FAIR. It is ; and duly signed and witnessed. (*Looks it over.*) Millions to char-
ity, but not so much to his only child as even the bare mention of her name.

NIGHT. Well, there's no use crying over spilt milk. Come, I say, let's get to
work and out of this.

FAIR. Why, you thieving bat, put up your useless kit. A single match is all the
tool we need to pick the bigot-guarded lock to all this unforgiving father's riches ; and
thus vanishes all record of the past, and from its ashes shall, Phœnix like, arise an
honest life. (*Lights match and sets fire to the will.*)

NIGHT. What noise was that ? (*Fairlook hastily crams the will into his coat
pocket. Nighthawk hurriedly glances into hallway.*) To cover ! To cover !
(*They conceal themselves ; but, in his haste, Nighthawk forgets tools lying on the
table.*

(*Enter* RUTH, *very cautiously.*)

RUTH. I'm sure I heard him come in some time ago. He must have gone to bed.
(*Looks about, sees Delmont, and draws back.*) No, there he is ! (*Advances cautiously.*) And sound asleep. Oh, fa—, but, no ! no ! I must not awake him—he
might curse me for it. (*Kneels by Delmont's chair.*) If I only dared to kiss his dear
hand, this parting might not seem quite so dreadful. (*Weeps ; gently lifts
Delmont's hand and kisses it repeatedly.*) Poor, poor, thin hand : how cold it is.
(*Looks at Delmont.*) He does not even seem to breathe. That's very strange !
(*Rises, looks at Delmont, and then disc vers the tools left by Nighthawk on the
table.*) What's here : Father ! Awake ! awake ! Speak to me ! (*Snatches handkerchief from Delmont's face.*) Great God, they've murdered him ! (*Staggers
and clutches table for suppo t.*)

NIGHT. (*Appearing and drawing a bowie-knife.*) Utter a sound and it will be
your last.

RUTH. (*Seizing the jimmy and springing between Nighthawk and entrance to
hallway.*) Villain, if you escape, it shall be only over my dead body. Help !
Murder ! Murder ! (*Nighthawk rushes upon her, but is met and grappled with by
Fairlook. They struggle fiercely.*)

NAN. (*Outside.*) Perlice ! Perlice !

NIGHT. (*Stabbing Fairlook, who groans and falls.*) I'll kill you all before I
will be trapped !

(Enter NANNY, *in her night-dress ; and armed with a brace of big, old-fashioned pistols, which she aims at Nighthawk).*

NAN. You'd better stand still right where you be. They're hair jiggers, and the slightest jar will turn 'em loose. Git behind me Miss Ruth! I'll stop him, dead sure.

(Enter POLICEMAN.)

POL. What's all this row about ?

NAN. You're one of the few early Blue Birds, and there's your worm. Sic him, Mr. Copper !

POL. *(To Nighthawk.)* Drop that knife and throw up your hands, or I'll let daylight through you. *(Nighthawk drops knife near Fairlook.)*

FAIR. *(Aside.)* I'm done for, but I'll do her one last kindness before I go. *Fumbles painfully and weakly for the will and a match, while Policeman handcuffs Nighthawk.)*

RUTH. Who is this assassin ?

NAN. Let's look at you. *(Tears off Nighthawk's mask.)*

RUTH. Nighthawk !

NIGHT. Yes, and not the only rare bird you have caught.

FAIR. *(Striking a match and trying to light the will.)* *(Aside.)* It's soaked in my own blood, and I cannot light it.

POL. What are you doing there ?

FAIR. Trying to make my last will and testament—that's all.

POL. *(Taking will.)* I'll take care of this.

RUTH. Who is this other murderer ? *(Attempts to remove Fairlook's mask.)*

FAIR. *(Feebly resisting.)* For both your sake and mine, spare me !

RUTH. Spare you ? I'd tear it off, though your eye-balls came from their sockets with it. *(Pulls off mask.)* My husband ! No ! No ! This night's awful work has driven me mad, and fills my reeling brain with cheating, hell-born visions ! My John ; my worshipped, honored husband ; my father's slayer and a prowling thief ? It is not he ! Some murderous fiend has stolen his noble semblance !

FAIR. With my last breath, I implore you to forgive me, Ruth, for, guilty as I am, I have loved you.

RUTH. Loved me ? Forgive you ? Why, so I ought. Sure'y such matchless love deserves some recompence. But favors too quickly granted loose their value. I will be generous with you, my noble, honest, loving lord and husband. *(Pointing to Delmont.)* When he forgives you, then I, too, will forgive you. When the frantic mother forgives the blood-stained savage who flings in her face the throbbing heart torn from her infant's breast, then I, too, will forgive you. When the snake-crowned sovereign of the hell that spawned you, and yawns to welcome your return with plaudits, learns honor, truth and mercy, I will go to him, that he may teach me to forgive you !

FAIR. Oh, remember I was your husband, and am a dying man !

RUTH. So I would have you, for it saves me from killing you ! My father cursed you, and, yet, what were his wrongs to mine ? You only stole his child, but you have robbed her of that father's love, her honor, hope and heaven. You only murdered him. *What have you done to me ?*

FAIR. Be merciful, for I swear to you I did not harm him, but found him as he is.

POL. He speaks the truth, madam. There are no marks of violence upon your father. He died a natural death.

RUTH. That's a most monstrous lie, and shall not serve to protect the guilty. Poor soul, he died a most unnatural death. There are two murderers here, and neither shall escape. *(Laying her hand on the Policeman's arm.)* But, good Mr. Officer, one of them is a woman : a very wicked woman, who killed her poor, old, loving father. Still she is a woman, and as such you may grant her one, small favor. Don't pinion her, and put the black cap on her guilty head, and the rough, strangling noose about her neck, first. *(Pointing to Nighthawk.)* Let her live long enough to see him hang.

NIGHT. Take me away ! Why do you keep me here ?

FAIR. Oh, Ruth ; my wife ; my only love ; forgive, for— *(Dies.)*

POL. He is gone.

RUTH. Gone ! Who's gone ?

NAN. Him as was your husband, dearie. Come with me ! Come away from this dreadful place.

RUTH. My husband gone ? Why, yes ; you remember, Nanny ! You heard him say that he was going, but would return by morning.

NAN. Alas ! alas, dearie ! That morning will never come.

26

RUTH. Why, Nanny, what do you mean by that? He has come back. I saw him but a few moments ago. Where was it? (*Looks around.*) Why, there he is now. But what does he there? (*Kneeling at Fairlook's side.*) Get up, my love! This is no time to sleep. Your clothes are damp, you most imprudent boy. You'll catch your death. (*Looks at her hands and screams.*) It's blood! It's blood! and they have murdered him! (*Picking up knife.*) And here's the knife that did the cruel deed. (*Rises and goes to Delmont.*) Father, avenge him! (*Looks at Delmont.*) What's this? Why, he's dead, too, and I killed him. Nanny, come here!

NAN. Yes, dearie; here I am.

RUTH. Listen! I once heard our good Rabbi preach from the text, "An eye for an eye, and a tooth for a tooth," and he said it was Jehova's revealed law. Then it must follow, a life for a life. Is not that so, Nanny?

NAN. I suppose so, dearie.

RUTH. (*Pointing to Nighthawk.*) The law will make it so in his case, and by the higher law it should be so in mine. A life for a life; and thus I yield mine up, a living sacrifice for all my sins. (*Stabs herself.*) Father, I've made atonement to the law. Forgive me! I come! I come! (*Falls dead at Delmont's feet.*)

[CURTAIN.]

www.ingramcontent.com/pod-product-compliance
Lightning Source LLC
Chambersburg PA
CBHW031800090426
42739CB00008B/1092